TIME FOR KIDS

BOOK OF HOW

ALL ABOUT SPORTS

TIME FOR KIDS

Managing Editor, TIME FOR KIDS: Nellie Gonzalez Cutler
Editor, Time Learning Ventures: Jonathan Rosenbloom

Book Packager: R studio T, New York
Art Direction/Design: Raúl Rodriguez and Rebecca Tachna
Writer: Curtis Slepian
Illustrator: Felipe Galindo
Photo Researcher: Elizabeth Vezzulla
Special Thanks to: Harry Chamberlain, Anne Jewell, Zane Martin, Donna Moxley Scarborough, Neil Soderstrom, Turkey Hill Dairy

REDESIGN BY DOWNTOWN BOOKWORKS, INC.
Project Manager: Sara DiSalvo

COVER DESIGN BY SYMBOLOGY CREATIVE
Designer: Mark Wainwright

TIME HOME ENTERTAINMENT
Publisher Jim Childs
Vice President and Associate Publisher Margot Schupf
Vice President, Finance Vandana Patel
Executive Director, Marketing Services Carol Pittard
Executive Director, Business Development Suzanne Albert
Executive Director, Marketing Susan Hettleman
Publishing Director Megan Pearlman
Associate Director of Publicity Courtney Greenhalgh
Assistant General Counsel Simone Procas
Assistant Director, Special Sales Ilene Schreider
Senior Marketing Manager, Sales Marketing Danielle Costa
Associate Production Manager Amy Mangus
Associate Prepress Manager Alex Voznesenskiy
Associate Project Manager Stephanie Braga

Editorial Director Stephen Koepp
Senior Editor Roe D'Angelo
Editors Katie McHugh Malm, Jonathan White
Copy Chief Rina Bander
Design Manager Anne-Michelle Gallero
Editorial Operations Gina Scauzillo
Editorial Assistant Courtney Mifsud

Special Thanks to: Katherine Barnet, Brad Beatson, Jeremy Biloon, Susan Chodakiewicz, Rose Cirrincione, Assu Etsubneh, Mariana Evans, Christine Font, Hillary Hirsch, David Kahn, Jean Kennedy, Kimberly Marshall, Nina Mistry, Dave Rozzelle, Matthew Ryan, Ricardo Santiago, Divyam Shrivastava, Adriana Tierno

Contents of this book previously appeared in Time For Kids Big Book of HOW.

For information on TIME For Kids magazine for the classroom or home, go to WWW.TFKCLASSROOM.COM or call 1-800-777-8600.

For subscriptions to Sports Illustrated Kids, go to www.sikids.com or call 1-800-889-6007.

Published by TIME For Kids Books
an imprint of Time Home Entertainment Inc.
1271 Avenue of the Americas
New York, New York 10020

ISBN 10: 1-61893-360-4
ISBN 13: 978-1-61893-360-7

"TIME For Kids" is a trademark of Time Inc.

We welcome your comments and suggestions about TIME For Kids Books.
Please write to us at:
TIME For Kids Books
Attention: Book Editors
PO Box 11016
Des Moines, IA 50336-1016

If you would like to order any of our hardcover Collector's Edition books, please call us at 800-327-6388. (Monday through Friday, 7:00 a.m.– 8:00 p.m. or Saturday, 7:00 a.m.– 6:00 p.m. Central Time).

1 QGT 14

Contents

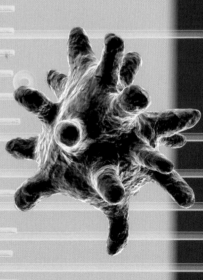

HOW Do Bicycle Gears Make You Go Faster?

A bicycle is a great way to get around. It doesn't pollute, it's easy to ride, it's good exercise, and it's fun. One of the best things about a bike is that you can make the ride smoother with the press of a lever. What allows you to get in gear is, well, the gears.

A gear is a wheel with teeth that stick out. A bicycle has two sets of gears. One set is connected to the pedal, the other is attached to the rear wheel. A three-speed bike has 3 gears, or "speeds." A mountain bike may have 24 gears. These gears let you change the distance the bike travels forward each time you turn the pedals. The higher the gear you put the bike in, the more distance you can travel with each turn of the pedals—and the faster you can go.

The gears are wheels with teeth, or cogs, that fit into the chain. As the gears move, so does the chain.

The back gears are turned by the chain. As the gears turn, so does the back wheel.

The rear derailer (derailleur) changes the back gears by moving the chain from gear to gear.

The crank turns the front gears.

The chain connects the front and rear gears.

Top athletes need to know the newest technologies, the best equipment for their sport, and the right moves. But you don't need to be a pro to learn some awesome sports skills.

Gearing Up

The higher the gear, the farther the bike goes each time it's pedaled. If the front gear on a bike is twice as big as the rear gear, the rear wheel will turn two times each time you pedal once. If the front gear is three times bigger than the back gear, the back wheel will turn three times for each turn of the pedals.

Bicyclists have to pedal harder in high gears, but they can go faster. Riders use high gears to go down hills or speed up on straightaways. In lower gears, riders don't need to pedal as hard, but they can't go as fast as in high gear. Riders use low gears to go up hills.

The **front derailer (derailleur)** changes the front gears by moving the chain from one gear to another.

The **pedals turn the crank.**

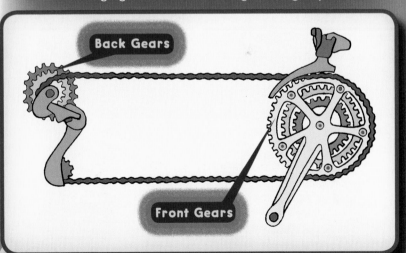

Back Gears

Front Gears

HOW Are Baseball Bats Made?

When major league baseball players grab a bat in the dugout, more often than not it's a Louisville Slugger. Louisville Sluggers are a big hit with ballplayers—and they have been since the company Hillerich & Bradsby began making wood bats in 1884 in Louisville, Kentucky.

There are dozens of bat companies in the U.S., Canada, and Japan. But Hillerich & Bradsby is the most famous. Over the years since the company's creation, it has sold more than 100 million bats. It sends about 200,000 bats to the pros each year. More than 60% of major league players use Louisville Sluggers, including David Wright and Evan Longoria. To learn how bats are made, you have to head home. Not to home plate, but to the home of the Louisville Slugger.

FACTOID

About half of all major league bats produced by Hillerich & Bradsby are made from ash trees, and the other half are made from maple trees. The company grows the trees in forests it owns in Pennsylvania and New York.

1 Every Louisville Slugger starts out as a log cut from trees at one of three mills in the Northeastern U.S. One tree can produce 40 bats. Inside the mill, machines remove bark from the logs, which are cut into 40-inch-long sections.

2 The logs are cut into 18 to 20 smaller tubes, called billets. Billets are damp, so they are dried out in an oven for four to five weeks. The billets are cut down to 37 inches, then shipped to the Louisville Slugger factory in Kentucky.

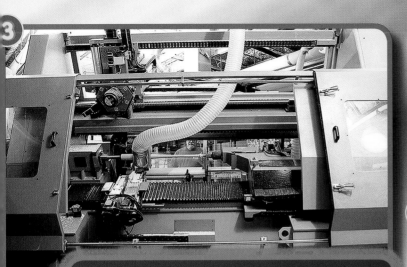

3

Major league equipment managers send in orders for bats. Players choose specific types of wood (ash or maple), shape, length, weight, color, and finish. A machine controlled by a computer shapes the billet into the correct bat model.

KEELER, N. Y. AMER.

5

4

A player can have his signature stamped on the bat with oil dyes. Or the signature can be burned on with a metal brand heated to 1,400°F. Machines then sand the bat and cut off the knobs, which were used to hold the bat in place.

If a bat is colored, it is dipped in paint and hung to dry. Once the bat stops dripping, a special light dries it further for 15 minutes. Now it's ready to be shipped to stadiums around the U.S. and Canada. An average pro player will go through about 100 bats each season.

HOW Does Hockey Equipment Keep Players Safe?

Ice hockey is a cool sport. It's also a rough game. Professional players can skate at speeds around more than 20 miles per hour. That's almost as fast as the fastest sprinters in the world. When skaters collide, bodies often crash against wood and glass boards surrounding the rink, or fall on hard ice. Players also shoot rubber pucks that can hit players. The hardest shots send the puck at speeds around 100 miles per hour. Players can get cut and poked by hockey sticks and skates. To avoid injury, ice hockey players cover themselves from head to toe in protective equipment. After all, staying safe should be every player's goal.

Mouthguard: Plastic guard that fits over the teeth. This helps protect the teeth from flying pucks and hockey sticks.

Gloves: Protect hands against an opponent's stick, the puck, and the sharp edge of skate blades. The outer part and finger area are thickly padded. The inner side is thinner, so players can feel and control the stick.

Skates: The outside of the shoe is a rigid shell, sometimes with metal mesh built inside it. This stops a skate blade from cutting through the shoe. The heel of the skate is rounded, not sharp, so it won't cut other players.

FACTOID

In most youth hockey leagues, players can't raise their sticks high or play too roughly. Hitting, or checking, another player with the body is not allowed.

Helmet: A hard plastic shell protects the head. Many helmets come with a plastic shield that covers the eyes and upper part of the face or a wire mask, or cage, that covers the whole face. Some helmets have a shield and a cage.

Shoulder and chest padding: Protect the collarbone, shoulders, chest, and upper arms and back. They are made of very hard plastic sewn onto foam-padded cloth. Some have extra pieces that protect the stomach area and lower back.

Pants: Inside are pads of cloth and plastic to protect parts of the leg, hip, and lower back.

Shin guards: Made of plastic, they protect the knee and the lower leg, right down to the foot.

The Man in the Mask

With pucks flying around at 100 miles per hour, what goalie wouldn't wear a face mask? Well, before 1959, no goalies did. The first to wear one in a game was Montreal Canadiens goalie Jacques Plante. At the time, people thought he wasn't very brave. Eventually, all goalies began to wear masks. Over the years, they have gotten larger to protect more of the goalie's head and throat. Players also decorate their masks. Here are some masks that have been worn through the years:

● The first mask, worn by Jacques Plante, was made of fiberglass and was held on by a strap.

● Early masks got bigger, to cover more of the goalie's face and head. Padding was also added.

● Goalies had trouble seeing out of their masks—until Soviet goaltender Vladislav Tretiak showed them how. The front of his mask was covered by a metal cage. Because the cage wasn't touching the face, being hit by a puck didn't hurt as much.

● In the 1970s, players began painting their masks. Today, the masks are like works of art.

HOW Do You Do a Skateboard Trick Called an Ollie?

In the 1950s, California surfers needed something fun to ride when there were no waves. So they invented the skateboard. The first skateboards looked more like scooters than today's models. They were made of metal roller skate wheels attached to a wooden board or box. Skateboarding didn't really take off as a sport until 1973. In that year, plastic wheels were first attached to skateboards.

Thanks to plastic wheels, skaters could go faster and do cool tricks, such as skating on two wheels (wheelies), spinning on the back wheels (pivot), or jumping over a bar and landing back on the board (hippie jump). In 1976, a skater from Florida named Alan "Ollie" Gelfand invented a trick that let the skater pop the skateboard into the air. Gelfand's invention opened the way for many mid-air tricks. His trick is the one most beginning skateboarders learn first: the ollie.

Q&A with Tony Hawk FROM TFK

Many consider **Tony Hawk** the greatest skateboarder of all time. TIME FOR KIDS asked him some questions.

TFK: What did you feel when you started out as a young skater?
Hawk: When I first went to the skate park, and I saw what was really possible— these guys were flying out of empty swimming pools—I was like, "I want to do that. I want to fly." So then I started going to skate parks on a regular basis. Every time I went, I would learn something new.

TFK: What advice do you have for beginning skaters?
Hawk: Take it slow. It takes repeated attempts to learn a kick flip and to develop skills. And you've got to work at it.

TFK: What advice do you have for kids who hope to achieve success?
Hawk: Do what you love doing, even if it doesn't seem like it's the coolest thing at the time. If you enjoy it, you have to follow it, because ultimately you're going to be happy going to work every day.

1

Put your front foot near the middle of the board, about two inches from where the bolt is. Your back foot should be on the tail, or back, of the board.

2

Bend both your legs and squat down. You should be ready to jump.

3

Slide the side of your front foot to the front of the board. At the same time, push down hard on the tail with your back foot. Your back leg should straighten as the tail hits the ground.

4

When the board is in the air, stop moving your front foot. Pull your knees up toward your chest. Raise your back foot so the board can rise until it is fairly level in the air.

5

When the board is level in the air and it begins to drop, straighten your legs.

6

As you land, bend your legs to absorb the shock. The board should be level as it lands, so all the wheels touch ground at the same time. Both feet should be over the bolts. Your back foot should not be over the tail. Don't try this on a moving skateboard until you have the trick down.

HOW Do You Do the Snowboarding Trick Called Butter?

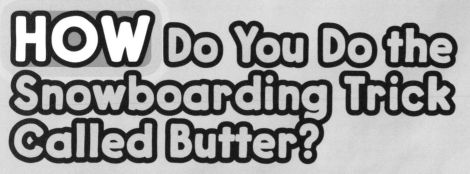

Do you like to shred? No, not cutting paper into small pieces. *Shred* is slang for snowboarding, a sport that's like skiing, but on one board and with no poles. Modern snowboarding was invented in 1965 by Sherman Poppen. He tied two cheap skis together and surfed down snow: He snurfed. When a better version of a snowboard was introduced a few years later, the sport became as popular as skateboarding.

Snowboarders jump, spin, and do wild midair tricks. Because a snowboarder's feet are attached to the board, jumps are easier to make. But you can do plenty of on-the-ground snowboarding tricks. One of the most basic moves is called butter, which lets a boarder easily spin in a complete circle. Butter can be done at low speed and on flat snow. When you finally have it down, it's, um, snow good!

Beautiful Boards

Snowboards not only go fast, they look great. The artwork on snowboards makes them really stand out in the snow. Here are a few awesome examples:

1 Find a flat, smooth, empty area to practice. The snowboard should be flat against the snow.

2 Put most of your weight on your front foot. Raise your back foot to lift the board off the snow. Don't lift it too high or you'll lose your balance.

3 As the board's tail rises, rotate your body, using your front foot as a pivot. Swing your back foot around until you face the opposite direction.

4 Once you've turned 180 degrees, put the tail of the board down.

5 Without raising the board, press your rear foot down hard on the snow. Rotate your body so the board spins on the ground back to your original position.

FACTOID

Some people claim that the creator of the snowboard was M.J. Burchett in 1929. He made a board out of a plywood plank, attached horse reins to the front, and used a clothesline to hold down his feet.

HOW Do Ice-Skaters Spin So Fast?

When figure skaters glide onto the ice, they perform beautiful jumps, twists, and turns. One of the most exciting parts of a skating program is the spins. Skaters start their spins slowly and end up looking like a blur. The faster a skater spins, the more she wows the audience—and the judges. There are all kinds of spins. In one kind, the skater spins in a sitting position. In another, she stays upright and may bend her back. In a spin called the camel, the skater spins on one leg while the other leg sticks straight out in a horizontal position.

Some skaters spin faster than others. They look like they're digging a hole in the ice! Swiss skating great Lucinda Ruh set a world record in 2003 for spinning 115 times on one foot—without stopping! Skater Robbie Robertson could spin at 500 revolutions per minute. That's how he got his nickname, "the Blur."

1 When the skater starts spinning, her arms or legs are held away from the body. That is like the Earth rotating on its axis. The axis of the skater is the vertical line that goes from the top of her head to the blade of the skate.

2 The skater begins to move her legs toward her body. That's because the closer the arms and legs are to the body, or "axis," the faster she spins.

3

She spins fastest when her arms and legs are tight against the body. Figure skaters control the exact speed of the spin by carefully controlling the movements of their arms and legs.

4

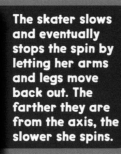

The skater slows and eventually stops the spin by letting her arms and legs move back out. The farther they are from the axis, the slower she spins.

One Good Turn

You don't have to have a pair of skates and an ice rink to increase your spinning speed. All you need is a swivel chair.

1. Adjust the seat of the chair as high as it goes. Sit in the chair with your arms stretched out to the side.

2. Start spinning the chair with your feet, or have a friend spin the chair—but not too fast.

3. Slowly move your arms over your head. What happens?

The Dizzy Factor

Spin around in place really fast and you get dizzy. You can hardly stand up. So how do figure skaters not get dizzy and not fall down when they spin 30 or 40 times in a few seconds? Well, most skaters do get dizzy. In professional ice-skating, there are small lights at each end of the rink. This helps a dizzy skater figure out where she is at the end of the spin. Some skaters say they just get used to the dizziness. After a while, it doesn't bother them. One skater says that if everything around him is a blur, he is less aware of the spin and doesn't get dizzy. Others just enjoy spinning—they think it's relaxing!

HOW Do You Stay Upright on a Surfboard?

Hang ten. Surf's up. Gnarly. Stoked. Surfing has given the world a lot of awesome terms. That's because surfing is a totally tubular sport. It's also a difficult skill to learn and master.

Catching a wave and riding it to shore isn't easy. The surfer's goal is to stay standing on the surfboard for as long as possible. Surfers do this by staying ahead of the white water of the wave—the part that crashes down. Some waves form a tube as they break. Experienced surfboarders like to ride inside the tube so they are surrounded by water. They know how to ride out of the tube before several tons of ocean fall on them. It takes years to become an expert surfer. But the first step is learning how to stand up on a board.

Catching Big Waves

Big-wave surfers are surfers who seek out monster waves, often 20 to 40 feet high—like the one shown here in Oahu, Hawaii. The biggest wave ever surfed was 78 feet high, ridden by Garrett McNamara in 2011.

FACTOID

The original surfers were Polynesians in the islands of the Pacific Ocean. They first rode wooden boards on waves about 3,000 years ago.

Surf's Up!

Standing up on a surfboard on water isn't easy. So practice on the beach or other dry land. First, figure out which position is more comfortable: right foot forward or left foot forward. Lay the board on a flat surface. Use a board that doesn't have fins.

1

Lie stomach down on the board. You shouldn't be too far forward on the board. Stretch out your arms and hold the rails, or sides of the board.

2

Slide your hands back until they are beneath your shoulders. Do a push-up: extend your arms to push your body up.

3

Get into a crouch. If you are a righty, bring your left foot forward. If you are a lefty, move your right foot forward. Your front knee should be lined up with your chin.

4

Stand up slowly, but not all the way. Keep your forward foot in the same position. Move your back foot so it's a few feet from the front foot. Remember: don't try this in water unless you've first taken lessons at a good surfing school.

HOW Can You Prevent Sports Injuries?

Playing sports is fun, but not if you overdo it. Young athletes often injure their bones, muscles, and tendons (tissue that attaches muscles to bones). A lot of these injuries are caused when athletes put stress on the same body parts over and over. This often happens when they play one sport and play it year-round. By the time young athletes are in middle or high school, nearly half of their injuries are caused by the wear and tear of overuse.

Athletes also get overuse injuries when they play different sports that stress the same body parts. Basketball and soccer players often have trouble with their knees. Divers, cheerleaders, gymnasts, and football players may develop back problems. Baseball and tennis players risk injuries to their elbows. For young athletes, a little variety and not overdoing it are good things.

On these pages are four common sports injuries young athletes get.

Baseball

Little League elbow: Slight tears and inflammation of tendons and ligaments in the inner elbow

Cause: Throwing too hard and too often, especially curveballs

Warning signs: A painful or stiff elbow when throwing a ball, difficulty holding arm out straight, pain when gripping or carrying heavy objects

Prevention: Kids ages 9 to 12 should not pitch more than four innings per game or six innings a week. Stop throwing curveballs.

Soccer

Sever disease: An inflammation of the back of the foot where the heel bone attaches to the Achilles tendon

Cause: Overuse of bone and tendons in the heel

Warning signs: One or both heels hurt while walking, running, or jumping.

Prevention: Gently stretch calf muscles daily and before games. Wear sports shoes with strong arch supports. Don't walk or run in bare feet.

Basketball, Volleyball, and Bicycling

Jumper's knee: An inflammation of the tendon that attaches the kneecap to the shin bone

Cause: Frequent jumping or doing intense activity that puts stress on the knees

Warning signs: Pain just below the kneecap that increases during physical activity, especially running or jumping

Prevention: Warm up before games. Let your coach know if you feel pain in knees. Rest between games or stop playing until pain goes away.

Running

Shin splints: An inflammation of muscles or tendons attached to the shin bone

Cause: Running downhill or on a slanted surface, running too hard, too fast, or too long

Warning signs: Pain, soreness, tenderness, and sometimes slight swelling along the front edge of the shin

Prevention: Run before season and slowly increase distance. Do not sprint while running for distance. Wear proper running shoes. Stretch calf and ankle muscles before and after competitions.

TFK TOP 5 Sports Kids Play

Do you play hoops, baseball, soccer? A poll of more than 1,000 kids reveals what their favorite sports to play are.

1. Basketball .... 30 %
2. Baseball .... 20.9 %
3. Football .... 20.8 %
4. Hockey .... 9.8 %
5. Soccer .... 9.1 %

Source: Sports Illustrated Kids

FACTOID

According to the National Council of Youth Sports, 44 million children take part in youth sports in the U.S. 66% are boys and 34% are girls.

HOW Does an Arena Change an Ice Rink into a Basketball Court?

Ice hockey and basketball couldn't be more different. Hockey players bang into each other as they skate on ice. Basketball players run and jump on a wooden floor.

Even though the games and playing surfaces are very different, the sports are often played in the same arena—and on the same day! How do workers make the changeover? Here's how it works in the Staples Center, located in Los Angeles, California.

3:49: The Los Angeles Kings beat the Boston Bruins, 4–3. The game went into overtime, so the Staples Center workers have less time than usual to get ready for an NBA game, which is set to start in less than four hours.

3:59: The crew first takes down the Plexiglas sheets around the rink. Forklifts help remove the sheets and the pieces that hold them place. Then workers begin to cover the ice with more than 600 panels, which protect the ice surface and help keep it frozen.

4:38: After workers cover the floor with panels, they put down the basketball floor. They start at center court and build outward. The basketball court is made of 217 pieces. The pieces are numbered and come out stacked on top of one another.

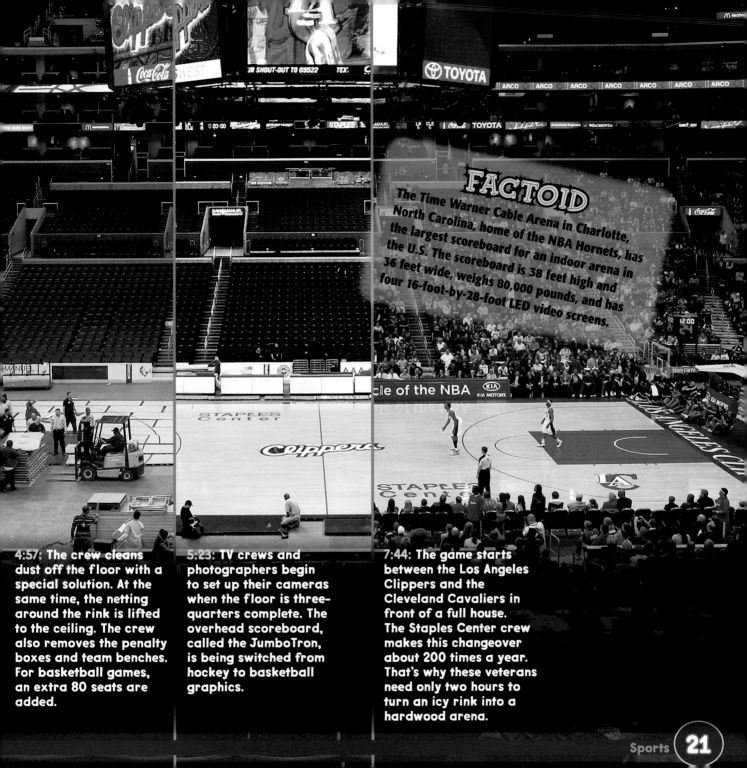

4:57: The crew cleans dust off the floor with a special solution. At the same time, the netting around the rink is lifted to the ceiling. The crew also removes the penalty boxes and team benches. For basketball games, an extra 80 seats are added.

5:23: TV crews and photographers begin to set up their cameras when the floor is three-quarters complete. The overhead scoreboard, called the JumboTron, is being switched from hockey to basketball graphics.

7:44: The game starts between the Los Angeles Clippers and the Cleveland Cavaliers in front of a full house. The Staples Center crew makes this changeover about 200 times a year. That's why these veterans need only two hours to turn an icy rink into a hardwood arena.

HOW Does Motion Capture Technology Help Athletes?

Motion capture technology is a way to make a computer-generated figure look incredibly lifelike. In motion capture, a person's movements are captured by cameras, recorded by a computer, and turned into a 3-D animation of that person.

Motion capture is capturing the imagination of sports teams. Motion capture is helping some major league baseball teams see what caused, or may cause, an injury to a pitcher. It is also used to improve players' performance.

A coach can compare the motion capture version of a baseball player when he is hitting well and when he is in a slump. Motion capture is also a tool to help athletes train.

A football team might create a motion capture animation of its linemen. Then a football player wearing 3-D glasses can practice against these life-sized animated teammates. Best of all, there's no chance of getting injured!

To make a motion capture of a pitcher, researchers attach 75 small globes, called markers, to different parts of his body. Above the pitcher are 20 high-speed cameras that capture him as he goes through his pitching motion. Each camera shoots out infrared rays that bounce off the moving markers and get recorded in the camera.

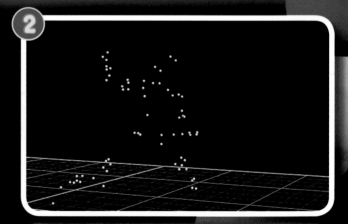

The images in the camera are sent into a computer. On the computer screen the player looks like a moving cloud of dots against a black background. Each dot is a marker.

3

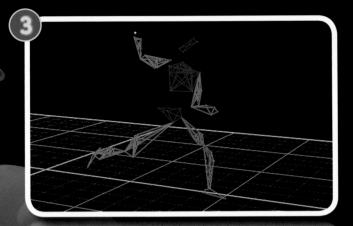

A software program connects the dots. Now the pitcher looks like a three-dimensional doll. The markers on the fingers, wrists, and shoulders are made to look like the doll's arm. It doesn't look like the pitcher, but it moves just like him.

Capturing Stars

From soccer to skateboarding, sports video games are using motion capture to make the animation more real than ever. To imitate the signature moves of famous players, video-game makers are giving more and more sports stars the motion capture treatment. Boston Red Sox second baseman Dustin Pedroia has been motion captured, and so have many NBA players, from Kyrie Irving to Chris Paul.

Some athletes have to really work out in front of the motion-capture cameras. Hockey player Rick Nash took 50 different shots on goal in a session. A group of English soccer players produced 150 different moves a day over five days. The results are worth the effort. Some games are so realistic, pro players watch them to pick up tips on how to improve their own—real—game.

4

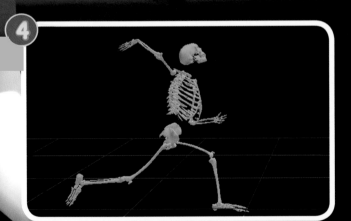

Researchers can make the image look like a skeleton. It lets them see the stresses placed on the body's joints when the pitcher throws the ball.

5

Researchers can also make the image look like a video-game version of the pitcher, complete with uniform and baseball cap. This makes the animated player's movements clearer to the athlete and coach.

HOW to Make a High-Bounce Ball

How are soccer balls, baseballs, basketballs, tennis balls, and Super Balls alike—besides being round? Answer: They all bounce. But how come a ball bounces? And why doesn't it keep bouncing forever when you drop it?

As an object drops, it picks up energy, called kinetic energy. When an object stops falling, it has stored, or potential, energy. As a ball drops, it builds up kinetic energy. When it hits the ground, this energy causes the ball to flatten. While the ball is motionless for an instant on the ground, it has potential energy. As it springs back to its original shape, it releases the stored energy as kinetic energy. So the ball bounces. No ball can bounce back to its original height (although Super Balls come close). The ball loses energy each time it hits the ground. And air resistance wastes more energy. Out of energy, the ball dribbles to a stop.

FACTOID

The largest Super Ball was the size of a bowling ball. It was accidentally dropped out of a hotel window in Australia. The ball bounced up 15 stories and came down on a parked car, destroying it.

What You Need

- 4-ounce bottle of white, school glue
- 1-pint glass jar
- 1½ cups distilled water
- Food coloring (any color)
- 2-quart bowl
- 1 teaspoon borax powder (a laundry detergent found in the supermarket)

What to Do

1 Pour the bottle of glue into the jar.

2 Fill the now-empty glue bottle with ½ cup distilled water. Then pour the water from the glue bottle into the jar.

3 Put 10 drops of food coloring into the jar and stir.

4 Pour the remaining distilled water into the bowl. With a parent, add the borax powder. Stir until the powder dissolves.

5 While stirring, slowly pour the glue into the bowl containing the borax.

6 Take the glue mixture out of the bowl. Push and pull on it until it's smooth and dry. Roll it into a ball and make it bounce.

How the Ball Bounces

Some people call it a bouncy ball. Others call it a power ball or Super Ball. Whatever the name, it's the bounciest ball ever. The original Super Ball was invented by Norman H. Stingley in 1965. He took some rubber, added a few ingredients, and heated it up under great pressure. Wham-O, the company that sold the Frisbee, produced the first Super Balls. Now many companies make these bodacious bouncers.

Some people claim a Super Ball is so elastic, it will bounce for a minute even if it's dropped from a short height. The first bounce of a Super Ball reaches more than 80% of the height it was dropped from. That's three times the height that a tennis ball reaches. When it first came out, people would slam a Super Ball on the concrete and watch it bounce higher than a three-story apartment.

What Happened

Fluids can be thin and flow easily. Or they can be thick and flow more slowly. The measure of a fluid's ability to flow is called viscosity (vis-*kos*-eh-tee). The thickness of some fluids changes when you apply a force. You applied force to the goopy mixture when you pulled and pushed it. This thickened the goop so it couldn't flow easily.

HOW to Find the Sweet Spot on a Bat

When hitters get "good wood" on a ball, they're hitting the ball on the "sweet spot" of the bat. It's the spot that makes a ball go farthest.

When a player hits a ball on the sweet spot, most of the energy the two moving objects produce goes into sending the ball toward the seats. If you hit the ball anywhere else on the bat, the bat will vibrate from head to handle. These vibrations waste energy, so less energy is transferred to the ball. The ball won't go as far as when it's hit off the sweet spot. Vibrations sometimes cause another problem. If you've ever hit a baseball off the handle of the bat, you know the vibrations can sting your hands!

What You Need

- Baseball bat
- Baseball
- Pencil
- A friend

What to Do

1 Between thumb and index finger, hold a bat about halfway down the handle. (Hold an aluminum bat about one-quarter of the way down the handle.) The barrel of the bat should point down.

2 Tap a baseball against the bat, right below the fingers holding it. The bat should vibrate.

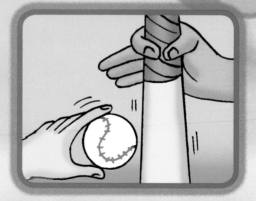

DID YOU KNOW?

Some players have "corked" their wood bats. They hollowed out the barrel and put cork, bouncy balls, or other light material into the hole, believing they could then swing the bat faster and create more power. Corked bats are not allowed in Major League Baseball.

3 Keep tapping the bat, moving down the barrel. Find the spot where the tapping doesn't make the bat vibrate. Mark the spot on the bat with a pencil. This is the sweet spot.

4 Hold the bat in a horizontal position and have a friend drop a baseball onto the bat from about a foot above it.

5 Drop it at different points along the bat. The ball will bounce highest at the sweet spot.

Going, Going, Gone?

When big leaguers come to the plate, they swing lumber. Only wood bats are allowed in the major and minor leagues. But in many youth leagues, players can use metal bats. And that worries some people.

Young players like metal bats because they let kids hit the ball harder. Metal bats are hollow, which makes them lighter than wood bats. This makes it possible for hitters to swing the bats faster. Also, metal bats are more flexible than wood, which causes the ball to bounce off them with greater force. There is worry that balls hit off metal bats travel so fast, they can injure infielders, especially pitchers.

Some people want metal bats outlawed. Others say metal bats don't cause any more injuries than wood ones. They also point to the cost. Wood bats break and have to be replaced. Metal bats, although more expensive, last much longer. Defenders of metal bats say players should wear more protective equipment. Or the fields used by young Little Leaguers, which are smaller than regulation, should be made bigger. That way, fielders will have time to duck. The debate continues. What do you think?

FACTOID

Not even Babe Ruth could have swung this bat. One of the largest bats in the world is 120 feet long and weighs 68,000 pounds. The six-story-tall steel bat is located outside the Louisville Slugger Museum & Factory in Louisville, Kentucky.

HOW Does the Stomach Digest Food?

If you gulp down too much pizza too fast, your stomach will expand. Nerve endings in your belly tell your brain, "You're full. Stop eating!" And you do—after having that one last slice. But what is happening to the pizza you've eaten?

The slices are taking a long journey through the digestive system. After you swallow, the food goes down a tube called the esophagus (es-*ahf*-a-gus). The pizza then makes a pit stop in the stomach. The stomach is a muscular bag that crushes the food and churns it in a strong acid until the pizza turns into a soup-like liquid called chyme (kym). The chyme sits in the stomach for hours, until it's ready to move on to the intestines and out the other end.

Check out how food gets broken down in the stomach (and learn why the stomach doesn't digest itself).

Mucous cells: These cells produce mucus, a thick liquid that coats the stomach lining and keeps the hydrochloric acid from touching it. The cells also produce bicarbonate. When this chemical mixes with the mucus, it turns the acid into water. Even if the stomach does get damaged by the acid, every cell in the lining is replaced every week.

The human body is an amazing, complicated machine. It doesn't come with an instruction book, but we know a lot about how the parts work and how to keep them running.

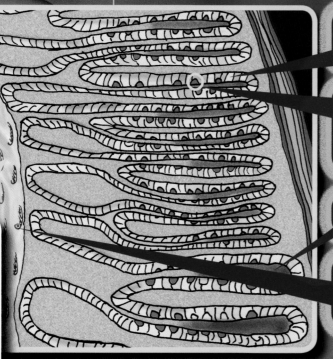

Pepsin cells: They produce a chemical called pepsin, which breaks down proteins and carbohydrates in food.

Acid cells: The hydrochloric acid made in acid cells turns food into liquid. Hydrochloric acid is strong enough to dissolve wood and even some metals. If too much of this is produced, it can irritate the stomach lining.

Gastric glands: Hydrochloric acid and pepsin mix in narrow tubes called gastric glands.

Gastric pits: The mix of hydrochloric acid and pepsin flows out of the gastric gland and into the stomach through millions of tiny holes called gastric pits.

The Poop on Poop

The solid waste that you flush down the toilet is made of a lot more than undigested food. What was once your meal is called feces (*fee*-sees). This is a mass of undigested food, dead cells that got scraped off the intestine walls, and dead bacteria. The large intestine contains lots of bacteria, which help digest food. When feces pass through the large intestine, they pick up the bacteria. It is these bacteria that give the feces their brown color.

When we eat something, a wave goes up and down the digestive system. This wave pushes the feces to the end of the large intestine and into a storage area for poop called the rectum. When the rectum fills with feces and stretches, sensory cells let the brain know that it's time to go to the bathroom. Muscles along the anus relax and allow the waste to exit the body.

HOW Do We Cry?

When you see a sad movie, you cry. When a piece of dust gets in your eye, you shed tears. Our eyes can turn into a water fountain pretty easily. Even when we're not crying, tears are constantly being produced. Every time we blink, we spread tears over our eyes. This type of tears is produced slowly and steadily. They keep our eyes smooth, clear, and free of bits of dust and pollen. Tears also keep our eyes healthy. They contain salt and proteins that nourish the eye, and a chemical called lysozyme (*lie*-suh-zym), which fights germs.

If an eye gets irritated, the tear glands produce a flood of tears. This can happen when wind, smoke, or fumes strike our eyeballs. People also cry when they are sad, happy, or in pain. Tears produced by strong emotions contain hormones produced in the body. Crying washes away these hormones—and sometimes makes you feel better.

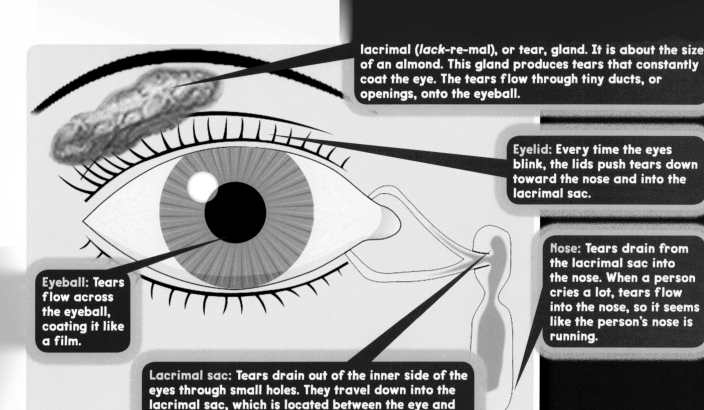

lacrimal (*lack*-re-mal), or tear, gland. It is about the size of an almond. This gland produces tears that constantly coat the eye. The tears flow through tiny ducts, or openings, onto the eyeball.

Eyelid: Every time the eyes blink, the lids push tears down toward the nose and into the lacrimal sac.

Nose: Tears drain from the lacrimal sac into the nose. When a person cries a lot, tears flow into the nose, so it seems like the person's nose is running.

Eyeball: Tears flow across the eyeball, coating it like a film.

Lacrimal sac: Tears drain out of the inner side of the eyes through small holes. They travel down into the lacrimal sac, which is located between the eye and the top of the nose.

Do Animals Have Emotions?

Humans aren't the only animals to shed tears. Most mammals have tear glands that work like ours to clean and keep eyes moist. But no one knows for sure if animals tear up from emotion. In fact, no one knows for sure if animals feel emotions. But more and more researchers are coming to believe they do.

Many scientists agree that animals feel pain, which is an emotion. But some animal experts believe they feel other emotions as well. An experiment showed that rats feel bad when they see other rats suffering. Gorillas seem to act sad when their child dies. Mother elephants appear upset when separated from their offspring. There are many stories of a dog acting unhappy when its human owner dies. One researcher claims that birds feel many emotions and another scientist says that even fish feel fear. However, many scientists say there is no proof animals have emotions.

HOW Do Medicines Work?

When you're feeling sick, you might need to see a doctor. After you tell the doctor what's wrong, the doctor will examine you. He or she will look into your eyes, nose and throat, listen to your heartbeat and lungs, and take your blood pressure. Armed with information, the doctor will offer a diagnosis—the reason why you are sick—and give a treatment. Often that treatment is some kind of medicine.

Medicine is a chemical, and it can come in many forms. It can be a liquid, tablet, or capsule you swallow. Drugs can be injected with a needle right into the bloodstream. Creams or ointments are absorbed through the skin. Drops are made for the eyes or ears. Inhalers spray a drug into the nose or throat. Drugs can fight an illness, prevent an illness, and make the symptoms of an illness less strong.

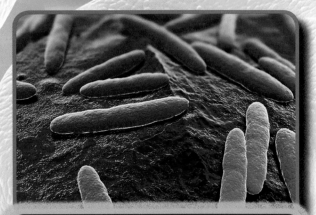

Disease fighters: An antibiotic kills bacteria or keeps them from multiplying. Bacteria (shown here greatly magnified) are germs that can sometimes cause disease. Certain drugs also kill other types of microorganisms that can lead to disease, such as fungi or parasites. Medicine can also target cells that aren't working normally, such as cancer cells.

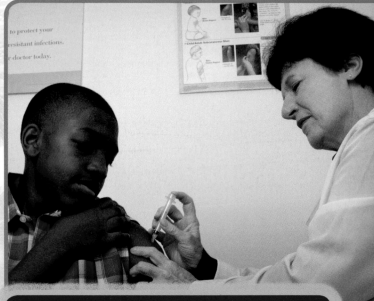

Be prepared: A vaccine is made of a dead or weakened part of a germ, such as a flu virus. When a vaccine is injected into a person, the body reacts by building up defenses for that particular germ. If that type of germ one day tries to infect the person, the body will be ready to attack it right away.

Perfect Timing

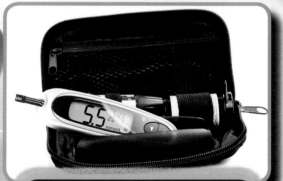

Pain killers: Pain killers like aspirin can make you feel better while your body heals. If a part of the body is injured, nerve endings send pain signals to the brain. The drugs interfere with the message, so the pain stops.

Some medicines are solid pills. The medicine dissolves all at once inside the body. For other medicines, it's important that they release their medicine slowly, so the body doesn't absorb it all at once. These are called time-release drugs. They are usually capsules that hold hundreds of tiny hollow balls, or pellets. Inside each ball is the drug. Some balls have a thin coating. These dissolve within an hour or so after swallowing and release their drug in the stomach. The drug goes through the stomach walls and into the bloodstream. Balls with thicker walls don't dissolve until hours later, after they reach the intestines. The medicine enters the bloodstream through the intestine walls. The balls are sometimes different colors, based on the thickness of the coating.

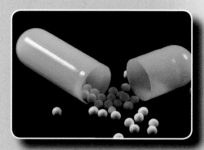

Replacements: Sometimes the body doesn't produce enough, or any, of a substance. Drugs can be used to replace those substances. For example, a person with a disease called diabetes needs extra insulin to stay healthy and gets it in an insulin shot. The shot comes in an insulin kit like the one in the photo.

FACTOID

One of the first drugs sold in tablet form was aspirin, in 1900. The chemical in aspirin comes from a substance found in willow bark.

HOW Do Eyeglasses Help Us See Better?

The eye is an amazing and complicated organ that starts working when light passes through the cornea. This is a clear shield over the eye that focuses light. After the light enters a small opening called the pupil, the lens focuses it again, but this time onto the retina at the back of the eye, where an image appears upside down. The retina is covered by cells that are sensitive to light. When light hits the retina, the cells send electric signals to the brain. The brain unscrambles the signals to make the right-side-up image that we see.

We take vision for granted, but our eyes don't always work perfectly. Some people have trouble seeing near or far objects clearly. If things are blurry, glasses or contact lenses may be needed. When we put them on, the world comes back into focus.

DID YOU KNOW?

● Ancient Babylonians and Greeks tried to see more clearly by looking through pieces of rock quartz. The crystal acted like a lens and focused light.

● Benjamin Franklin invented the bifocal lens around 1760. These allowed a person to see clearly up close and at a distance through the same pair of eyeglasses.

The Eyes Have It

To keep your eyes healthy, follow these tips:

○ Eat five servings of fruit and vegetables every day. Nutrients in foods such as oranges; broccoli; corn; carrots; and green, leafy vegetables will help keep your peepers perfect.

○ Get plenty of exercise. Physical activity gets the blood moving, which delivers more oxygen and nutrients to your eyes. But be sure to protect your eyes with goggles if you play contact sports.

○ When on the computer, look away for 20 seconds every 20 minutes to avoid eyestrain. Don't sit too close to the screen. Your eyes should be about two feet away.

○ Get an eye exam by a doctor at least once every two years.

Focus on the Eyes

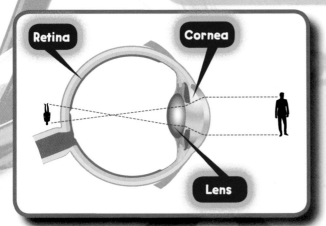

Farsighted: A farsighted person can see objects at a distance clearly. Things that are close look fuzzy because either the eyeball is too short or the cornea is too flat. Light from near objects focus behind the retina, not on it. Glasses or contact lenses that correct this are convex—or "curve out slightly," which makes the light spread apart and focus on the retina.

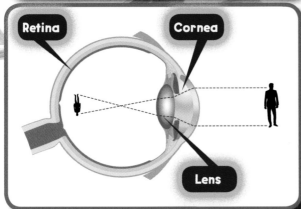

Nearsighted: Nearsighted people see close objects clearly. Objects that are far away are blurry because the eyeball is too long or the cornea curves too much. The light from distant objects focuses in front of the retina. Glasses or contact lenses that correct this are concave, meaning they curve in slightly. This makes the light bend in and focus on the retina.

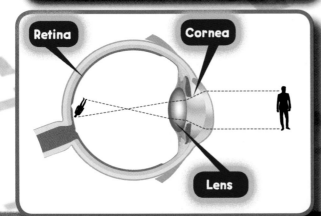

Astigmatism: A person with astigmatism (ah-*stig*-ma-tiz-im) may see objects both near and far out of focus. The cornea of most people is shaped like a baseball. With astigmatism, the cornea looks more like a football. Light scatters, focusing on different areas of the retina. This makes objects seem wavy. To correct this problem, glasses and contact lenses focus light on the same area of the retina.

HOW Does the Body Fight Germs?

Germs are all around us. Most are harmless, but a few can make us sick. When bacteria, viruses, and other microorganisms (tiny one-celled life forms) try to infect us, our immune system springs into action. To be immune is to be protected, and the immune system has several ways to fight germs and keep us healthy. The first line of defense is our skin, which keeps out germs. The natural openings in the body, such as the mouth and eyes, produce chemicals to kill germs. If germs do get through our outer defenses, they are attacked by different types of white blood cells.

When we are infected, we feel sick: glands in the neck or armpits get swollen and tender, our temperature rises, skin that is cut may get red and sore. These are signs that our body is battling the germs.

Chemicals in saliva and in **tears** fight bacteria.

The surface of the skin is full of dead cells, which don't give germs a foothold. The skin also produces chemicals that can kill some bacteria.

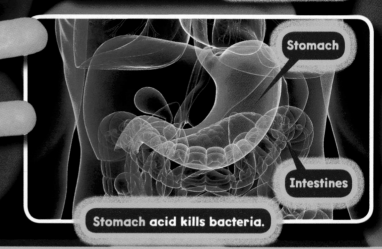

Stomach

Intestines

Stomach acid kills bacteria.

Mucus in the nose can trap germs.

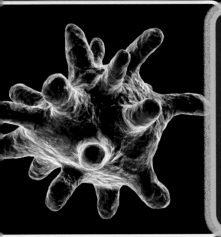

White blood cells, including macrophages (*mac*-roh-fayj-ez), are in different organs and also travel through fluid in the lymph (limf) system and in the blood. They patrol the body looking for germs to swallow and kill. These cells are so small, they can only be seen through powerful microscopes.

Keep Healthy

The immune system works hard to fight off germs and keep you healthy. But there are ways you can pitch in and help out your body's defenses.

● **Get enough sleep.** You should be getting 9 to 10 hours of sleep every night.

● **Eat right.** Try to eat three regular meals of nutritious foods that include fruits, vegetables, and whole grains. Avoid sugary foods and drinks, as well as fast foods. Drink plenty of water.

● **Exercise.** When you exercise, you strengthen your bones, muscles, and heart, and make the lungs work better. Being active burns off extra fat, and it helps you digest food. Do anything that makes you move—even walking is good for you and your body.

● **Reduce stress.** Too much stress over a long period of time can weaken the immune system. Talk over your problems with your parents or teachers. To reduce stress, exercise, develop hobbies, read for pleasure, or play with a pet.

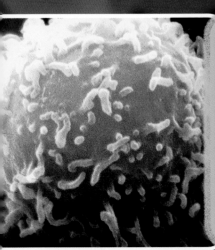

This photo, taken by an electron microscope, shows a special type of white blood cell called a lymphocyte (*lim*-foh-site). Some lymphocytes produce proteins called antibodies. The antibodies stick on germs, so other white blood cells will know to kill them.

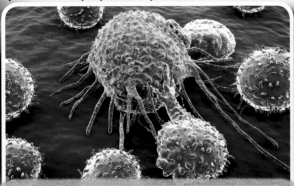

This computer-generated image shows white blood cells called killer lymphocytes (the blue balls). As they travel through the body, they search out and attack cancer cells (the yellow ball), as well as germs hiding in cells.

HOW Does Loud Music Hurt Your Hearing?

You've probably heard that listening to iPods and MP3 players through earbuds at high volume can hurt your hearing. Unfortunately, people who hear the warnings don't always turn down the volume. Some people think the maximum setting on an iPod is safe. But at the highest volume, some music players are as loud as a chain saw or rock concert.

Researchers have found that listening with earbuds or in-ear headphones to music at full blast for just five minutes a day can, over time, cause permanent hearing loss. Listening at a high volume an hour a day can damage your hearing after five years. So when you're listening to music, turn down the volume.

Auditory canal: Sound enters through the auditory canal and is funneled to the eardrum.

Eardrum: Sound makes the eardrum vibrate back and forth like a drum.

FACTOID

The tiny bones of the middle ear—the hammer, anvil, and stirrup—are the smallest bones in the body. They stay the same size throughout a person's lifetime.

Ossicles: The vibrating eardrum shakes three ossicles (*ah*-sic-uls), or tiny bones. Because of the way they look, they are called the hammer, anvil, and stirrup. As they move, they push and pull a membrane at the beginning of the inner ear.

Inner ear: This contains the cochlea, as well as the semicircular canals—the part of the ear that controls balance.

Nerves: They carry electrical signals to the brain.

Cochlea: The cochlea (*koh*-klee-ah) is filled with a fluid that vibrates when the ossicles vibrate. Those vibrations reach an area that contains 15,000 to 20,000 tiny hairs. The fluid makes the hairs bend. As they bend, they send electrical signals through nerves to the brain. The brain "hears" the signals as sound. Loud noise can damage or kill hair cells, and that causes hearing loss. Once the hairs die, they don't grow back.

Sound Advice

This chart shows how many decibels different sounds produce. A decibel is a measure of a sound's loudness. Any sound above 85 decibels can, over time, damage a person's hearing.

Sound	Decibels (db)
Lowest sound that can be heard	0
Breathing	10
Mosquito	20
Whisper	30
Refrigerator hum	40
Normal conversation	50–65
Laughter	60
Vacuum cleaner, hair dryer	70
Motorcycle	90
Train, garbage truck	100
Snowmobile, jet overhead at 100 feet	105
Drill, jackhammer	105
Jet taking off	130
Rock concert	140

HOW to Make a Stethoscope

Lub-dub, lub-dub, lub-dub. That's the sound a doctor hears when she listens to your heart through a stethoscope. The heart has four flaps of skin, or valves, that open and close as blood pumps through them. The lub-dub sound of a heartbeat is actually the noise the valves make when they open and close. You can hear the sounds if you put your ear to someone's chest. But a stethoscope makes the sound much clearer.

On one end of a stethoscope is a plastic disk, or diaphragm (*die*-a-fram), which is pressed against a person's skin over the heart. Sounds make the diaphragm vibrate. The sound waves travel up two tubes, through the earpieces, and into the doctor's ears. A doctor uses the stethoscope to hear if the heart is beating normally. If you want to hear what your doctor hears, make your own stethoscope.

What You Need

- 2 small funnels
- Rubber or plastic tubing (a cut up piece of garden hose, for example)
- Tape or glue
- Scissors
- Rubber band
- Balloon
- Timer

What to Do

1 Fit the rubber tubing into each end of the two funnels. Tape the tube tight to the funnel.

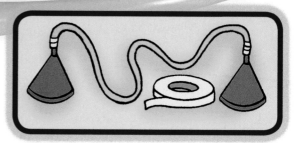

2 Blow up the balloon in order to stretch it out and then let the air out.

DID YOU KNOW?

The human heart beats about 100,000 times during one day, 35 million times a year, and about 2.5 billion times in a lifetime.

3 Cut off the balloon about one-third of the way up from the opening. Throw away the part with the opening.

4 Take the balloon and stretch it over the wide opening of one of the funnels. It should fit tightly. Hold it in place with a rubber band if the balloon slips off the funnel. You can use the stethoscope without a balloon, but the balloon makes it easier to pick up sounds.

5 If you can't find one or two funnels or tubing, make your own. To make the funnel, cut out a six-inch-by-six-inch square of paper. Cut off one corner along a curved line. Roll the paper into a tube and tape it closed.

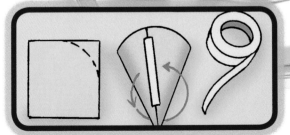

6 To make tubing, roll up a long piece of paper into a tube shape. Cut a piece off the tip of the funnel large enough to fit the tube. Tape the tube to the funnel.

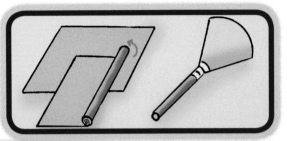

How to Use It

1. Feel your heartbeat with your hand. Your heart is located slightly to the left of the center of your chest.
2. Place the end of the funnel with the balloon over your helart. The funnel should press against your chest.
3. Put the other end of the funnel up to your ear. Listen for a soft beating sound. Count the number of beats you hear in 20 seconds. Multiply that number by three to calculate the number of beats your heart makes in one minute.
4. Run for a few minutes or do some other exercise and then listen to your heart again. Compare the results.

HOW to Find Your Dominant Eye

About 90% of people write, eat, and throw with their right hand. That means their right side is dominant, or in control. About 10% of people are dominant on their left side. Some people use their right and left hands equally. They are ambidextrous (am-bih-*dex*-trus). Some researchers think people have a dominant side because one side of the brain may be more dominant than the other side. But no one knows for sure why people are righties or lefties.

The hand isn't the only part of the body that can be dominant. To find out which foot is dominant, check out which foot a person kicks a ball with. Or which foot a person lifts first when climbing stairs or puts down when stepping on something. An ear can also be dominant. It's usually the ear a person uses to listen on a phone. Even an eye can be dominant. To find out which one of your eyes is dominant, try this experiment:

What to Do

1 Put your arms straight out in front of you. Your palms should face forward.

2 Make a triangle by overlapping your fingers and thumbs. Bring your hands closer together until there is a small opening, about the size of a quarter. You should be able to see through the triangle with just one eye.

3 With your arms held straight out, look at a small object in your room or an object in the distance through the opening you made with your hands. Stare at it with both eyes open.

4 Keeping both eyes open, slowly move the triangle back toward your face. As you do this, make sure the object is still in the opening. When the triangle nearly touches your face, note which eye it is in front of. That is your dominant eye.

5 If you want to double-check that you've found your dominant eye, try this: Look at the object again through the little triangle made by your hands. Keep your hands and head still. Close your right eye. If you can still see the object through the triangle, it means your left eye is dominant.

6 Now open your right eye and close your left eye. If you only see your hand, but no opening, your right eye is dominant.

Left Is Right

Since right-handers outnumber left-handers, lefties might feel a little, well, left out. Living in a right-handed world can be challenging for left-handers. It's harder to press the buttons on a watch worn on the right wrist. Remote controls and microwave controls are placed for righties. Most scissors are hard for lefties to use, and CD cases are difficult to open. But you have to hand it to lefties: many of them have gone on to greatness. Here are just a (left) handful of famous left-handed people.

- Bill Clinton
- Ronald Reagan
- John McCain
- Alexander the Great
- Henry Ford
- Bill Gates
- Barack Obama
- Bart Simpson and his creator, Matt Groening
- Leonardo da Vinci
- Angelina Jolie
- Eminem
- Cliff Lee
- Isaac Newton
- Helen Keller
- Babe Ruth

Glossary

ambidextrous able to use both hands equally well
antibiotic a medicine that kills bacteria
antibodies proteins in the body that fight off disease and infection
astigmatism the inability of the eye to focus light because the cornea doesn't curve normally
axis a straight line around which an object turns

bacteria microscopic single-celled organisms found in water, air, and soil
borax powder powder or crystals used to clean clothes

cells the basic structure of all living things; in a beehive, six-sided structures made of beeswax that store food and house growing bees
chyme food that has been turned into a liquid-like mass in the stomach
cornea the clear area that covers the front of the eye and focuses light
crystal a substance formed when atoms or molecules are arranged in a pattern that repeats

decibel a unit used to measure loudness
derailer (derailleur) a device on a bicycle that shifts gears by moving a chain from one gear wheel to another
diaphragm a thin disk that vibrates and produces sound waves
dissolve to mix a solid substance with a liquid until it is included in the liquid
distilled water water that has been boiled and condensed to remove any salts or minerals

electron a tiny particle that moves around the nucleus of an atom
esophagus the tube that passes food from the mouth to the stomach

farsighted an inability to see close objects clearly
fungus a type of organism, including yeastm molds, and mushrooms, that is neither a plant nor animal

gear a wheel with teeth that turns another wheel with teeth, so the motion of one controls the speed of the other
gland a cell or group of cells that produce a substance that a body uses or gets rid of

immune system cells, proteins, and tissue that protect the body from infection and disease
infection the invasion of the body by a microorganism, such as a virus, that causes disease
inflammation pain, swelling, or redness in the body caused by infection or an injury

joint the part of the body where two bones are connected

kinetic energy the energy of movement

lens the part of the eye that helps bring rays of light into focus

ligament tough tissue that connects two bones

lymph system the tissues and organs that produce and carry cells that fight infections

mammal a warm-blooded animal with a backbone that has hair or fur and feeds milk to their young

membrane a thin layer of tissue that covers, separates, or connects areas of the body

microphage white blood cells that play a role in the immune system by killing bacteria and other cells that enter the body

microwave electromagnetic radiation, similar to radio waves, that is used in microwave ovens to cook food

mucus a thick fluid that coats and protects the nose, throat, lungs, and other areas of the body

nearsighted an inability to see objects in the distance clearly

pepsin a chemical produced in the stomach that helps break down proteins for digestion

pollen a powdery substance produced by a flower and used to fertilize another flower

pollution the contamination of air, water, or soil by harmful substances

potential energy stored energy

protein a substance basic to living cells and necessary for an organism to function; it is an important source of energy in a person's diet

pupil the opening in the center of the eye through which light enters

rectum the lower part of the large intestine

retina light-sensitive tissue located at the back of the eyeball

solution a uniform mixture formed when one substance is completely dissolved in another substance

tendon tissue that connects bone to muscle

vaccine a medicine made of dead or weakened germs that prevents a person from getting sick from that germ

virus a tiny particle that can cause different types of illnesses by entering a person's body through the nose, mouth, or breaks in the skin

viscosity the ability of a fluid to flow or not flow easily because of its thickness

Credits

All illustrations and diagrams by Felipe Galindo unless indicated otherwise.

Cover: Mark Wainwright/Symbology Creative (background); Olga Besnard/Shutterstock.com (ice-skater); EpicStockMedia/Shutterstock.com (surfer); Dan Thornberg/Shutterstock.com (baseball); Alhovik/Shutterstock.com (bats); Pressmaster/Shutterstock.com (hockey player).

Back cover: Mark Wainwright/Symbology Creative (background); (Tony Hawk); Tuullaa/Shutterstock.com (crutches); Nicholas Piccillo/Shutterstock.com (baseball player); Matusciac Alexandru/Shutterstock.com (biker); Mark Wainwright/Symbology Creative (book covers).

Interior: 1: Mark Wainwright/Symbology Creative (background); Olga Besnard/Shutterstock.com (ice-skater); leonello calvetti/Shutterstock.com (mucous cells); Shkurd/Shutterstock.com (hand); R. Gino Santa Maria/Shutterstock.com (boy with basketball). 2–3: Zhana Ocheret/Shutterstock.com (background). 3: Peter Weber/Shutterstock.com (baseball player); Sebastian Kaulitzki/Shutterstock.com (macrophage). 4–5: Andrey Yurlov/Shutterstock.com (background); steamroller_blues/Shutterstock.com (bike). 6–7: Monkey Business Images/Shutterstock.com (background). 6: Kletr/Shutterstock.com (lumber mill); Al Tielemans/Sports Illustrated (machine). 7: Al Tielemans/Sports Illustrated(billets); Louisville Slugger Museum & Factory photo © Hillerich & Bradsby Co. (metal brand); Library of Congress, Prints and Photographs Division (Willie Keeler); Al Tielemans/Sports Illustrated(drying bats). 8–9: Pavel L Photo and Video/Shutterstock.com (background); Lebedinski Vladislav/Shutterstock.com (hockey player). 8: PhotoStock10/Shutterstock.com (mouthguard). 9: Nicholas Piccillo/Shutterstock.com padding); George Silk/Time & Life Pictures/Getty Images (Jacques Plante); Robert Riger/Getty Images (Vladislav Tretiak); William Melton/Shutterstock.com (painted mask). 10–11: Baronb/Shutterstock.com (background). 10: Robert Cianflone/Getty Images (Tony Hawk). 12–13: Ipatov/Shutterstock.com (background); Alex Ciopata/Shutterstock.com (snowboards). 14–15: Maxim Tupikov/Shutterstock.com (background); Olga Besnard/Shutterstock.com (ice-skater). 15: Paolo Bona/Shutterstock.com (ice-skater). 16–17: Gustavo Miguel Fernandes/Shutterstock.com (background). 16: Mana Photo/Shutterstock.com (big wave). 18–19: muzsy/Shutterstock.com (background). 18: Peter Weber/Shutterstock.com (baseball player); CLS Design/Shutterstock.com (soccer player). 19: Brian Chase/Shutterstock.com (runner); R. Gino Santa Maria/Shutterstock.com (boy with basketball); Tomasz Trojanowski/Shutterstock.com (boy on bike). 20–21: John W. McDonough/Sports Illustrated (all). 22–23: Courtesy of Donna Moxley Scarborough, MS, PT & Eric M. Berkson, MD of the MGH Sports Performance Center, Department of Orthopaedics, Massachusetts General Hospital (all). 24–25: bezmaski/Shutterstock.com (background). 26–27: Richard Paul Kane/Shutterstock.com (background). 27: Coprid/Shutterstock.com (metal bat); Louisville Slugger Museum & Factory photo © Hillerich & Bradsby Co. (Louisville Slugger Museum & Factory). 28–29: Creations/Shutterstock.com (background); leonello calvetti/Shutterstock.com (mucous cells). 28: new vave/Shutterstock.com (boy); Sebastian Kaulitzki/Shutterstock.com (stomach). 30: Lane V. Erickson/Shutterstock.com (crying). 31: Courtesy of FML/Erin Silversmith (eye); pokku/Shutterstock.com (gorilla). 32–33: Sebastian Kaulitzki/Shutterstock.com (background). 32: Sebastian Kaulitzki/Shutterstock.com (bacteria); CDC/Judy Schmidt/Shutterstock.com (doctor). 33: voylodyon/Shutterstock.com (white tablets); Dmitry Lobanov/Shutterstock.com (insulin kit); africanstuff/Shutterstock.com (yellow pill); Havoc/Shutterstock.com (willow tree). 34–35: Bomshtein/Shutterstock.com (background). 34: Library of Congress, Prints and Photographs Division (Benjamin Franklin). 35: Peter Hermes Furian/Shutterstock.com (all). 36–37: argus/Shutterstock.com (background); Gleb Semenjuk/Shutterstock.com (nose). 36: Shkurd/Shutterstock.com (hand); Blacqbook/Shutterstock.com (eye); Sebastian Kaulitzki/Shutterstock.com (stomach). 37: Sebastian Kaulitzki/Shutterstock.com (macrophage); National Cancer Institute/Dr. Triche (lymphocyte); Juan Gaertner/Shutterstock.com (killer lymphocyte and cancer cell). 38–39: zwola fasola/Shutterstock.com (background); Oguz Aral/Shutterstock.com (inner ear). 39: dwphotos/Shutterstock.com (concert). 40–41: Sashkin/Shutterstock.com (background). 42–43: Dhoxax/Shutterstock.com (background). 43: Ivelin Radkov/Shutterstock.com (coin); Official White House Photo by Pete Souza (Obama); Dfree/Shutterstock.com (Jolie); Library of Congress, Prints and Photographs Division (Ruth). 44–45: Zhanna Ocheret/Shutterstock.com. 46: Guilu/Shutterstock.com. 47–48: Zhanna Ocheret/Shutterstock.com.

Index